ALL TIMES EASTERN

PAUL VARGAS

OMNIALITY

BROOKLYN | 2014

Copyright © 2014 by Paul Vargas
All rights reserved
Printed in the United States of America

Library of Congress Control Number: 2014903520

ISBN 978-0-9916072-4-2

OMNIALITY
www.omniality.com
info@omniality.com

ALL TIMES EASTERN

PREFACE	13

33/45

I NEED THE REMOTE IN CASE THINGS GET BAD	17
RUNNING STEADY	18
SOUTHPAW	19
WAVEFORMS	20
DORIS	21
MANHATTAN	22
TENTH AVENUE	23
FIGHTS AHEAD	24
LAKEVIEW	25
ELEGY FOR B.	26
SELEUCIA PIERIA	27
1A	28
TREMENDOUS	29
POPPIES AS THE AUTHOR'S PHOTO	30
BELLS	31
WHITE FUR COAT IN A BATHROOM MIRROR	32
SEA BEACH LINE	33
BATTERY GRASS	34
WELLING	35
CLEANSING FLIGHT	36
EIGHTH OF A SONG	37
ALL TIMES EASTERN	38
ONSET	43
PREFECT A	44
PREFECT B	45

THIS SHELTER SO MUCH MORE

LIMN	49
MARKSON NUMBER ONE	50
DIRT-AND-CRABGRASS FIELD	51
PART OF THE INDUSTRY	53

MARKSON NUMBER TWO	54
WHIP	55
CAPE ANN DRIVE TIME	56
MARKSON NUMBER THREE	57
DE NUEVO EL VIEJO	58
IRRIGANT	59
MARKSON NUMBER FOUR	60
SECOND EPOCH, DURING WHICH WE SHARE OUR FEELINGS	61
THIS WISH FOR A FORT GREENE FRIEND	62
MARKSON NUMBER FIVE	63
E#	64
M STREET	65
MARKSON NUMBER SIX	66
A WORD	67
APAMEA	68

OCCASIONED BY YOUR THIRTY-SEVENTH

PART ONE	73
PART TWO	74
PART THREE	76
PART FOUR	78
PART FIVE	80

ALABAMA LOT

RATIONAL	85
SUB ROSA	86
LATAKIA	89
CHILD	90
ELEGY FOR A.	91
CHURCH	92
AN AFTERNOON	93
DEE DEE SHARP	95
ON THE EZEKIEL STANTONS, PLAYING LUDLOW	96

MULES MAY HAVE HORNS	97
CRAVES MISTAKES	98
AIRS	99
NOT BIG ON CELEBRATING	100
WAGGED	101
HERALDED	103
SWIFT	104
A LAST GOODBYE AT WINDSOR LOCKS	105
PSALM SUNG WITH HANDS	106
NERVOUS	107
WE PARTY AND BULLSHIT	108
SAVOY	109
INDELICATE DEMANDS	110
SEPULCHER	112

LOW LOWLY

ON THE RADIO YESTERDAY	117
NEXT TIME	118
ANTIOCH	119

Brooklyn
I love you
I'll be home soon

PREFACE

I am late to your party.
The guests have gone and
the bed's been freed
of wool and tweed.

Let me just wash that
last glass and grab a
dreg of the darkest rum
you've got. Sit with me;

sit, and tell me how
you sprinted in your youth.
Do you run still?
No, I don't,
not me;
not in two handfuls of years.

You can leave the lights off
everywhere but above
the stove. I can see your
photos from here, you friend.

Sometimes

sometimes I forget how tall you are.

33/45

Blood dries brown. Love lies loud.
Loud like plaid. Cool it down.
Slow it up. Mess around.
Up it goes, down in rules;
glad it's found sounds above—
drown in mud.

I NEED THE REMOTE IN CASE THINGS GET BAD

He had a wee nip of the beggar
on Rum Row; "Good God," he said,
"I love your dress,"—and pardon me
but that mess was much worse than just bad.

I had the piccolo put on mute,
and like blasting in with borrowed guns
Sheriff and I scattered the horse race:

Sandy was careering
like a freight train off-track;

Jill was a child
with big eyes, ticking;

but Lucy sat cornered, pleading
for more whipcrack.

Sandy and Jill blew the bash; took the bread.
We dropped our arms, and so as trash were taken,
only to hear the piper back on. Lucy continued,
the only one in any shape; we hear she placed.

RUNNING STEADY

A soldier lounging on a tank,
kaput outside Riems, pulls
from a bottle of red. He says,
"I just drive 'em. I don't fix 'em."

Wars of the chest. Marathons
are referendums on lust.

Great works kill us.
Slave-crafted pyramids.
A bridge over the mouth
of the New World, with six dead
in its caissons. Three torched,
desperate for the moon.

No loss is denied in the abstract,
but neither has progress been,
in the bowels of pursuit.

SOUTHPAW

Whisper to her,
though she's an almost
perfect stranger.

"The later it gets,
the lighter it gets,
the smaller
and safer
and quieter yet."

WAVEFORMS

I am heartened
by lights bright on
a shifting boulevard,

and heartened too by
that road's base changes:
proud; mad; brash
through crashes, dips,
and bashes.

I'm heartened by crown waters
gifted Whitman; later, seen
swamped by crafts fleeing
a deafening madness.

And I am struck dumb today,
awed by the simple fact
that more than just
a token few came back.

DORIS

Let Doris shine your shoes.
She needs the work,
and is easily impressed.

MANHATTAN

Sold on this concept of cool air
and the famous
in boat hats and dark shades

clutched close to a lover's
purple legging'd strut.

TENTH AVENUE

You've gone on swimming
and the skin of the bold blue tile

that's the floor of the pool

is warm to the touch
of the sole of your foot.

FIGHTS AHEAD

Smell that world! Seaweed
and dirt, thick to mouths.
Call me that taste: burnt like dogs.
Keep me near. It's Saturday,

and I'm in a mood
to spot some first-class villains.
Come on. Come and kick my ass.

As long as you all swear you've read
every book, and swear you'll speak
all the words, I won't mind
your strikes in the least.

LAKEVIEW

Heat was simple once.
Now a day scalds, with notions
as hideous as countdowns
and their nonsense virtue.
Nature spits on minders.

Summer spoils into fall,
and warmth is just
a nighttime proposition

negotiated finely, its will sanded
with high-grade grit. Faults grow
as tortured murmurs do, like

buying the broken.
A quaver is a craving:
for graying, upset dawns;
churned, unkempt hair.

ELEGY FOR B.

Knowing the dead, good man.
Laughs enough to shake a ribcage.
Leave a face aching.
Leave a note in the casket.

Remember always that such a thing
happened, among enough people to
smile and be seen. Remember that
we all left notes, and moved on,

poorer, but not as much as we'd feared.

SELEUCIA PIERIA

Wind seizes me.
This body's older. Thicker.
Mind's slow along currents
of children bold, running for
the snow.

Slowed, slurred. Ticket home.

Once I'm relieved of the burden
of memory, I may be frightened,
or may just recall a burden and
be relieved. So relieved.

Children spilling down a flight.
Snowball fights; they've no way
to retreat to the woods.

Better to steal onto sloops
and boat off to sea.

This body's thicker; older.
Cheap whiskey pangs and pings.
My fault. My and mine. Fine, really.

When I've drunk, I rhyme.
I recall the burned. I am so relieved.
I can see for miles and miles and miles.

The children only see across the street:
they man their posts; prepare their lobs.
Fire; volley. Fire; volley.
The sea, somehow, at all their backs.

1A

Pond-pocked marsh;
flatlands never so green.
Warmth of sunned wood,
gray and splintered.

Saltboxes, their faces due East,
and chilled to pain some nights.
The brick of Lynn: even sounds
are muted by the weather here.

Rumbles mumbled, brakes sighed.
A heavy E faces me,
quarried, paste-painted.
And past that, blue loud on

tin stacks but through window gauze.
The ride toward witches and bastards
marked by three white ducks
and Earth as seen by cottonmouth.

TREMENDOUS

Stood in that rented place
with him in his cups.

I'd not ever done
much—whatever's "ever"—
save pour this proud father
another snort and listen

to his pride and ingenuity,
braced by the will of an army,
and cash.

"Build a factory
in the Middle East,"
he told me,
"and when you can't make
the right concrete,

you ship sand to the desert."

POPPIES AS THE AUTHOR'S PHOTO

Words in a font
as perfect as your letters
on French-ruled paper.

Rolling Amish with
a couple weeks' worth
of handprint copies.
"Monk's work, indeed."

I'll run back
with a bonefolder
to crease our pages—
together craft a beaut.

BELLS

The belfry's weathered
and on this day
we can see clear to Calais.

May we have breakfast,
to smile upon the privilege?

WHITE FUR COAT IN A BATHROOM MIRROR

Like hell you've got foghorns near you.

If I remember right, your house
is just up the street. Bear no ill will
toward North Lamborn, and you'll see
Beattie and her tire swing soon enough.

But make no mistake: your
rivers don't so much die a death as
simply cease, and those early,
mournful bleats are just freight
passing through.

I fear I'd just be passing through,
too, but on my way to a clearing
with a view.

SEA BEACH LINE

Little boy with flour-blanched
wax-wrapped bun, chewing
piece-of-this, piece-of-that:

give the blue-white glow a
chance to endear itself.
Give brick and steel
time to settle sway.

Don't be a Given.
Everything here is temporary:
fortunes; arrests; the Big
that no one thinks but all'll
soon see; the Small that's
a nagging pea.

Respect a soured man,
and consider him a caution.
Respect love when it comes.
Consider it a caution.
Hate sleep as long as possible.

Learn a beaming grin at
a dour smile. Earn, then share.

BATTERY GRASS

I want dusk chained to me
and a humid press.
A grass patch underfoot.
I want what it takes
to build an hour
to crescendo
and give it to my friends.

WELLING

We took all these shots
the day before,
in the still air before dark,
when sound wouldn't carry.

A parking lot from a catbird seat,
a man full of mincemeat and regret,
but neither cook nor priest.

The hill; the town through
tinderbrush below. Clouds'd rolled
into eclipse and the clearer
sky stood, neither blue nor orange.

It was gold.
Stunning gold,
fury gold,

out from behind
a black engine.

It was a half-boundless
flame, licking up for more.
It was miserable lividity,
like shame prepaid.

CLEANSING FLIGHT

The bees waited until spring
for their cleansing flight,
and the child heard
it looked like poisoned rain.

The child told Mother,
and begged her to bring
the sheets in from the lines.

The child knew it wasn't poison,
but didn't want "to lay in shit."

EIGHTH OF A SONG

No one I know hasn't suffered, you know/

                                      Yet you've hardly
                                      had it the worst/

You're first to roundly murder your thirst/

                                      And then laugh at
                                      all sides 'til they
                                      burst.

ALL TIMES EASTERN

Tell the one about
when you woke up.   I often wake up.

Tell the one about
when you woke up and found
you'd slept on a sink
with a running faucet.   My pants were
                                        around my ankles
                                        and I'd lost myself
                                        down the drain.

There was ice on the floor.   I'd left the window
                                        open for hours.

And it was cold?   There'd been
                                        a blizzard.

What did you do?   I pulled up my
                                        pants and left.

~

Tell the one about
when you woke up.   That often happens.

Tell the one about
when you woke up but you
were bleeding.   I ached at my shin.

A fence'd cut you.   I'd caught one in
                                        Midtown.

But you walked? Six miles, once I knew, before I had to stop.

What then? I had to stop.

~

*Tell the one about
when you woke up.* I've yet to not.

*Tell the one about
when you woke up and she
was crying.* A strange man followed her; she ran home.

You held her. Was often that afraid myself.

Did she leave? Many times.

But here? We made love, and slept.

~

*Tell the one about
when you woke up.* Years and counting.

*Tell the one about
when you woke up and you
raced to the subway.* It was summer, but I was late.

*A man watched
the train approach.*

Older, swinging his arms. Timing.

You were the closest to him?

Until he wasn't the closest to me.

What next?

I shouted for a worthless ambulance.

~

*Tell the one about
when you woke up.*

All my stories start that way.

*Tell the one about
when you woke up but she
was already awake.*

She'd whispered at me all night.

Arguing.

Her face folded at the furrow in her brow. Sometimes it was permanent.

Did she leave, too?

Each time for good, and the fault was always mine.

And yet?

She'd come back, angrier.

~

Tell the one about
when you woke up.

...Tell the one about
when YOU woke up.

I once awoke.

You awoke and saw
a woman you loved.

Yes, but a friend.

She was gazing
kindly.

I'd arrived after a long trip,
and had parked in her driveway.

You drove a
convertible?

Very American; the sun
shone on my face.

What happened?

We listened to good radio;
we listened for hours.

~

Tell another.

I once awoke.

Keep going; it's
winter.

I once awoke and
our bags were packed.

The trip was
a surprise.

We traded papers we read
as we waited for our flight.

The trip would be
long?

*Six legs, at least; all we took
was time.*

                              And so?

*We washed the newsprint
off our hands.*

~

                              Don't tell another.
                              You're too well-off.

Perhaps you shouldn't sleep.   I tried that once.

*Perhaps you should go
for walks instead.*

                              I've watched the city
                              rise; I've watched
                              it go to bed; I've
                              watched it at all
                              times Eastern.

Many small moments of peace.   Not for me; I itch
                              and ache. Bastards
                              scald, and the
                              wounds need
                              treating.

You're equipped?   I have words; you
                              know I have older
                              pain. And I have
                              patience.

And when they've run out?   I expect I'll learn
                              to live in the cold.

ONSET

I've holes
as big as this rumble,
I've disappointments.

I've Victorinox slashes
and the extant desire
to sleep 'til noon.

Outrage I'm told I always
was supposed to have,
so do, and always had.

My flannel does my voting
for me. And my peace runs
toward its killers, their dull

penknives a nickel/salt
cancer. We'll meet again
in forty years, as the waters
repossess, but I expect

I'll be shrieking then.
Investigation contemptible
to hell and back,

half-dead, half-buried, all bloat
and bluster. All tumor-lymph,
like blood in urine.

PREFECT A

The explosion is a danger-
close harsh whisper.
The animals feel it, too.

In this same
damn fever dream,
the usual sounds mutter
the name "Turcius," but
a line like gibberish teases
glyphs, turned over and over
by wise—if weary—hands.

Translated upon waking:

> There
> are their legs and there
> are their arms and there
> lie their spines: spurned;
> mad—ravenous
> for that hand, two fingers
> outstretched, touching
> the trigger—creeping; seizing
> raw. Awaken, and bring
> a needle and thread; I can't
> sew those grimy cuts but
> the light's no longer perfect
> to split the eye, at any rate.
> There's too much smoke in here—

PREFECT B

Dreamt I scooped you up
and ran in wrong shoes,

yet could see your eyes
downcast at incorrect

perspective: a Vermeer
reflected. I could pick

your chin up with
my finger, and lead you

again to kill me, but we
were fleeing, and late,

and a mottled snake with
a raptor's head and twin

tails sped after us on four
short, stubby feet.

Since I'm now awake,
let's count our parts and give

thanks before getting on with the
business of hating each other.

THIS SHELTER SO MUCH MORE

Sun's run is done—
fun, but done. A
blunt shun of the one
come to hang in love.
Shoved who came to
turns above; whose
tons and tons of
fire won. Over,
lovely; brilliance: none.
Later, money; thieving
guns. Ask through acrid
billows spun.

LIMN

And now that word lies everywhere.

I'd pay a staggering ransom to
crack that ochre, paint with leaf,
to line that frame with lead;
I'd pray to make it heavy.

Lord, make it heavy, make it bright:
make it unmoveable in desire; in practice.
Make it so clear that it sings in
three complementary keys

yet make the bass rumble,
like lines of cannon 'gainst the beach.

MARKSON NUMBER ONE

Willie Tasby once played Baltimore center field shoeless for fear he'd be struck by lightning.

The metal cleats would have conducted the energy straight through to the ground.

DIRT-AND-CRABGRASS FIELD

Engines spent,
they tumbled out,
and staggered up the hill
to rest.

The loudest rode bitch. He
leaned in. Mercilessly
mirthful. A gasping
flare before the end of air.

Brothers. Born too profane to piss.
Four, young just that morning
and divers daring, never not
muttering of some win, some

girls. But *this* long day cooled
with nothing affirmed
save bruises, and hot patches
on their knees.

Pings still rang with their loss.
Heels of hands were worn; red-
raw pads by the knobs, too,
swinging; near-hitting.

Too long a time before pulling
endless, sweaty wallows,
glumly by the seawalk rail,
slow and low, before

the car came. They unwilling to go.
Though their heads ached; their vision
stung with dust. Though no chance
for victory. Just more age.

But at last, their hurled empties
met the sea. They filled
and faded, bobbed and blinked,
and sunk below the ebb

of tides knocking even
against tankers lying locked
in their berths,

their horns
booming back, back.

PART OF THE INDUSTRY

The glossy rags
are there to teach.
Bury your noses.
Study those poses.

To buy in, learn
what snakes crave
then sneak in stunts
that'll grant a second
to pull white streaks
on fair skin.

Consider them parlor tricks.
But seconds make minutes.

And minutes make hours,
so stunts make men.

MARKSON NUMBER TWO

There is no old saw about better angels and lesser mortals.

So says Remember Baker.

WHIP

Bow and arrow,
fields and low-power
static: a hockey
stick tinfoil-wrapped
and duct-taped to the
remains of a weather vane.
Out before the door,
a nine-foot plywood harp,
never tuned,
always supine.

CAPE ANN DRIVE TIME

Accident of birth,
stare down the cat
and blast some Somali
pirate rock. This one
comes from Moktab
and the Mellow-Tones,
and is fine, fine, fine:
number four with a
bullet. Lead's on the
hambone; a Rickenbacker
crown's dissed by
its mere suggestion.
We've got your life
raft here on the hertz,
rigged with a motor.
But it only seats three,
so someone's gotta float.
(And the cat can't swim.)

MARKSON NUMBER THREE

In the fifteenth century, Sherwood was *scherewode*.

Other haunts: *Yngil-wode* and *Barnysdale*.

No beaches. To Dover for those.

DE NUEVO EL VIEJO

Al principio, lloré,
y el hijo de ese familia
me miró, curiosamente.

Creo que voy a encontrarlo
de nuevo: mas viejo, y sin
esa curiosidad

que solamente me hizo
llorar mas duro,
sin verguenza,

por la noche que era
singular, y despues,
que fue desapareciendo—

oscuro a nada—
corriendo con alegria;
corriendo siempre.

IRRIGANT

Besides the beeping,
there's this flimsy pitcher:
urine-yellow with a cloudy lid
and in it, this stuff
that tastes like vermouth,

which is to say
that drinking vermouth
is akin to hearing you
groan in agony
while the next guy over
watches cartoons full blast.

MARKSON NUMBER FOUR

Dolley Madison ordered Stuart's portrait of George Washington saved from the advancing British.

The men from New York who saved it being warned not to roll up the canvas they pulled from the broken frame.

SECOND EPOCH, DURING WHICH WE SHARE OUR FEELINGS

If I could bring you to the beach,
and if you liked the beach,
and if I liked the beach,
then we would probably
like the beach.

If we could do silence,
there'd be silence.
As long as it was night,
and cool, and the breeze
smelled of salted grit.

We wouldn't mind grit
in the dark, and if we wouldn't
mind it in the dark,
we certainly wouldn't mind it
between our toes.

It's simple; it goes no further.
But I'm a misreader and
you're a misreader,
so let's misread these
same words together.

Like so:

if I save you too in many ways,
then I also save you in too many ways.

THIS WISH FOR A FORT GREENE FRIEND

Gold and gray,
nestled, rustled,
nose and poke

or better yet
white, brown, and black,
wet and warm,

and perfect-sharp,
click-floored, baying
(once on a full moon)

chipper at the buzzer,
lounging, lying,
pulsed and thrummed.

MARKSON NUMBER FIVE

Fante, of Edna Pruitt: how the Roper kids rooted through her trash for stillborn embryos.

E#

Little wing!
A sly grin to greet
the day and winter's
shot out of bed

to bare feet on
dirtdull boards. To
the same places fly—
once warmth's charm's

charred sharp
like smoke. Stay sane
on heels' brittle bones,
and keep splintered

those sighs and burns.
To build a new day.
To cover with a sheet,
and pine for spring.

M STREET

All this volume before us,
and our chests just won't expand.
Wrapped in blankets drenched with sweat;
the sheet corners always tied
to wouldring sticks, then twisted.

MARKSON NUMBER SIX

There are six possible combinations of the words "it's," "me," and "sugar."

Marilyn Monroe needing forty-seven takes to deliver the correct one for Billy Wilder.

A WORD

I believe
you are the type to spell
it "mannikin."

APAMEA

I am unwelcome
so I am gone
and if you should
see me again
it'll only be when
your milk is made warm
and your companion
made dumb and done.

OCCASIONED BY YOUR THIRTY-SEVENTH

"Down one" doesn't
if the *when* is *why*.
Blythe walks the edge
of Absinthe Main
and figures she is spry.
Murder every watch;
give them both your word:
those gibbons flocked as one
upper platform rafter bird.

PART ONE

Deep in those kudzu lands;
so are our arms bound
by vine, and thick vocal fry
I keep calling "freesh"
sits eight-legged on our
chests, housefly black,
choking breath.

You are big and sweaty,
bearded despite yourself, and
I am burnt,
invective mutterings growing
less and less frequent
as my paused tape frays.
What do I want before I go?

Not to've come down here,
only to be overrun by these snaking
tendrils and ivy-broad leaves,
and be dive-bombed by these
glottal horrors. This is less than
my idea of fun. This is Death,
marker-scrawled on a swelling balloon,

my asthmatic lungs pulling
those letters apart despite themselves.
To spite us. To buzz and whine
and slice us.

PART TWO

Add to our usual hangover
that slow, chuckling realization
that any post-mortem
would occur during a morning
of eggs and bacon,

postponed to two and a lunch of
burgers and fries, then five
and a dinner of wet pasta
and thin sauce, then seven
or seven-thirty, and a half-sleeve
of Ritz.

Then more long, low chuckles.
"Where did I get these bruises,
and where, GOD, is Hot Dog Girl?"

Oh, clap your hands like
a dirty old man
and tell me 'bout the
kingly thirst slaked by another
bath in moonshine. Been here

ticking like a schoolroom clock
since eleven, with shades shut on
dwarves shoving their rough-hewn
logs shaped into bed frames
and chairs out higher windows
for a laugh.

Soy-plastic beds made by soy plastic dwarves
who sweat booze in the heat of the night.
Don't tell ME we're missing a *Twilight Zone*
marathon; my nightmare is waking up
and finding the Earth is exactly where
they left it.

PART THREE

When we started,
our promise was fine,
I think.

I don't mean recently but rather
those days when you
drove a Jeep, and I spent nights
sleeping against a berm.

That sounds heartier
than it was. Hotter than Hell
then, too, and still bug-choked.

How many billions of insects
have we killed since then?
How many spiders have
we swallowed? I can't tell
if dementia happened
because of it or before it.

You're a forced Essene and
I'll be there soon enough, and
we're pockmarked by the
deaths of friends
and, moreover, strangers.

We're not confirmed.
Never, I expect, will we
ever confess. We've
deleted our baptisms.

What we're doing here
is being unoriginal, again,
for everyone who came
and all who've yet to come.

PART FOUR

Nor am I blameless.

I am blameful, blameish;
the willing receptacle both of
incipient blame and blame
in full bloom—spring blame—
that in the summer turns this
sort-of always-on blame such

that you can't even believe
that, even as the days grow shorter,
that this moody city sunset
light of blame won't last forever.

I bear fall blame's brunt like
Armstrong's gutterance at
the end of his notes, and the first
truly chilly daybreak. I'm on for
Christmas blame and Hanukkah
blame, and then

I'm your man for each and every
burst of blame, in every season,
until there are no more seasons.
Toes cold at three-thirty blame.
Rainbow ice burn on the back of
the tongue blame. Horn bleat
at the wind-wrecked corner
of Atlantic and Flatbush blame.
Blame on the subway; blame on the
streets; blame in the trees, desperate
to drop.

Or I am at the equator of blame,
from zenith to nadir
and nadir to zenith, held on the
Y-axis as I churn my legs sideways.
But I take nothing away from you.
I think we'd be brothers even if
all we shared were running shoes.

PART FIVE

So as we hang suspended,
let's make a pact:
that should we free ourselves
we'll truly be so,

as we'll have suspended
our hangings and bought
some more life. You, and me,
and our respective loves,

out by the lake or up by the bay
or down by the river: let's be
smarter than we were once younger;
let's be wiser. Let's work, and

be kind. If we're to live, let's do
it, and leave the plans
to the mortgaged, the pain
to the craven.

I mean to say next all I ever mean to say.

I mean to say I know.
I mean to say this shame is matterless,
and even after years lost,
we can succeed.

ALABAMA LOT

Seven-odd dirty Chevys,
nose-to-trunk on rusted
grass, windows shattered,
shat upon; tires blown
and gas tanks bled. Faintest
hint of heinous cherry scent,
on velour, though elsewise
wet from mildew creep
sealed in vents.

RATIONAL

The stunted man
declares on a gravel path—
forking behind him
in every direction—

"Empedocles once said there will
always be too many Mouths to feed."

In fact, the Greek said no such thing,
probably. But this one here's built
of broken glass and nonsense.
Bitten, yes, and boorish, grabbing
strange as if it were his due.

His monologue's an
improvisation beat by
his wet brain,
out his mouth. Starved, as
he's too taken with his seminar
to bother to eat.

SUB ROSA

In all this, I don't mean *you*.
I've never meant *you* and
could never mean *you*.

For you are fine; you
have always been fine and always
will be fine.

You are bright and talented; you
have always been talented and bright and always
will be bright and talented.

You are entitled to your opinions and
have always been entitled to your opinions and always
will be entitled to your opinions.

But moreover, your opinions are right. They always
have been right and always
will be right.

But *they* are wrong. *They*
have been wrong and *they* always
will be just plain wrong.

I don't know how they could argue with you; why they
have always been arguing with you and always
will argue with you.

I don't know why they're making you snipe; why they
have always made you shout, and always
will make you snap.

Fear not, though, for you are a SURVIVOR. You
have always found friends and always
will have more friends than those

you cannot hate, because you
are incapable of hatred and
have always been incapable of hatred and always
will be incapable of hatred.

Even though they speak in coded language; they
have trafficked in insinuation and always
will be willful.

You know you are entitled to what you take. And you
have always been owed what you take and always
will deserve more than you could ever take.

When you're taking, know that you're showing them. They
have been waiting for you to show them and always
will wait for you to finally show them.

In a civil way.
In an educated way.
In a way that shows you're truly unique.
In a leaderly way.
In an early-adopter way.
In a way that boosts all the good

and bans all the bad.
That censors. Bellows 'til it's cowed.
That shuns.
That won't abide dirty dissent.
That will fake before it offends.
That would sooner move the Earth itself!—

That'd sooner move the Earth from Offense than ever admit
that your level might have even ever been level with theirs.

For you are fine. You are bright and talented and have always
had opinions and always will be right and I don't know why
they're doing this to you and have always made you snipe, but
you always will be a SURVIVOR and have never hated and
you always knew they used code words, so you earned what
you took and have always been showing them and always will
be fine.

Thank you for being strong. I love you for being strong.
Let me grab you by the shoulders and whisper loud
in a tone I hope you think is beautiful,
"I LOVE YOU FOR BEING STRONG."

You are better than my own loving could ever be, and
have always been the only love I could ever need and always
will be my goddamned everything. Come here and show me
everything that I've been doing wrong.

Give me just enough to want more everything, like you
have always given me a taste of everything and always
will give me just enough everything.

When I am saying some bad thing, please censor me.
When I have made the wrong friends, please shun me.
Promise when I'm uncertain you'll never abide me, please.

For you are fine.

LATAKIA

Your relief is well-coined:
I can watch you chip at that
marble field for hours,
revealing smooth river stone;
revealing soft woods with a
series of miserable left turns.

And that trench-digging
you do leaves a mudpile
plinth, or pedestal, or priapic
monolith, rough-hewn and
graphite-burned
that can see no further
than ordinary fucking rocks.

Toss and catch the snipe;
your braying is music
wrought of clay.

CHILD

Apron strings:
tug them tight
so she can look down
and see you.

Wail. Wail louder
and harder than ever;
than you ever will—
embarrass yourself

with the wringing
contortions of stomp
and drop. You know
as well as I

that you can feel
embarrassed. Our
memories are long—
they're strings

dragged across that
grimy floor. They're
gray snow. City soot.
Country dirt.

ELEGY FOR A.

A brief note of apology:

I did not come to see you because
you weren't really there
the time I saw you last,

and if we were far enough apart
that you had faith in me,

then we were close enough
on how we see this world.

Belief in the bereft
is a cold way to put it,
but when we next see each other

I may tell you
that I should've believed salvation
comes not from holy men,

but sideways, from the selfish
and the dead.

CHURCH

The brass function
of pipe on marble
marvels.

Women with
absurdly large foreheads:
beluga in cotton-poly;
sweaty from the rain.

And this Jack Lord clone,
practiced at meeting all
gazes and none,
recruits as he eulogizes.

Good to have a body
at the organ; the keyboards
are a marvel.

No one set adrift
amid the seven parts
played will admit to
drowning the tune.

AN AFTERNOON

Flannery's

A fine kickoff: toasting to a lesser-known
Ivory Joe Hunter track. Left when glare
of noonday sun hit our window. Flannery
is dead.

McLaughlin's

Passable lagers. Burger reported overdone;
chicken moist as all get. We swore with love
at the Mets. McLaughlin is plenty alive;
he's the cook.

"Couch Bar"

Three Guinness apiece. Beating life
with swift kicks and strong liver swings.
Eco called a ponce; Hegel a killjoy. Left
when soul music was replaced with "neo-soul,"
which just sounds like Nina Simone
dead from dirty works. Couches lumpy,
but welcome.

Grassroots

A pitcher apiece. Flung a coaster
at people I can't call *hipsters* because,
despite their ubiquity, I'm told
hipsters don't exist. Approaching confessional;
shots hurried Episcopalian tendencies.
No grass; no roots. Plenty of hipsters.

Cab

Flask passed between us. Little said.
Window down; sun on my face like
when I fled a tiny, joyless sophomore,
and rode the old B train home.
The word *cab* means nothing to me.

The Way Station

Whiskey in stemmed glasses;
John Prine wailed between choruses
of "Camptown Races." The station
is a damned metaphor.

DEE DEE SHARP

Vinyl'd melt in real pop and hiss
but tonight it's just this
plastic-rubber bit, slipped over ring
and hit with the needle,

so that through well-worn cones
comes the wail of a woman named
Dee Dee,

and before long she pleads seven times
(or seven hundred,
or seven hundred million)
to be set at ease;

her pine on the word "heart"
containing all the vowels,
and as many syllables.

ON THE EZEKIEL STANTONS, PLAYING LUDLOW

If they get any louder,
the walls may bleed.

Surely, that mechanical bull
will rock off his post,

and charge into the crowd,
pell-mell and goring most.

Good for the bull;
bad for business.

MULES MAY HAVE HORNS

A mistake bears the tusks
of a white elephant,
the horns of a mule
(I suspect that, in
the metaphysic, mules
may have horns);

it crushes, with
braying, slimy, scaly
tonnage the gathered
angels on the heads
of pins, and spins.

CRAVES MISTAKES

Glass-footed
thin pigeon
gasping from a
smoky taste;

all stood-up slopes
on the face, always the
same acute angle.

Loves that half-break.
Craves mistakes.
Bends attacks with
wrongish language
then puckers

thick, searching lips,
bared;

sometimes bared teeth.

A glass-footed pigeon
climbing, sinking,
screaming silent with
mawp agape.

Shuttered lids and
serpent circles,
base-to-point 'til
boring bone.
Bared again.
Seared rouge.

AIRS

I still can't get your name
right. But we're mutually minor.
It's either you or me
who'll fade to a point

like that on the back of your neck
or the side of my face,
one pressed against the other,
huddled, you swear, this only night.

NOT BIG ON CELEBRATING

Look at these sliver-brass meals,
under glass. Listen to this racket.
So far, I've heard a fight and a fit,
but no pith or wit.

And I smell Ribena.
Ribena! Lousing stout.

This is a land God forsook. These
people don't live—they lease. Errors'll roll
into drunken, bookish, mumbled *oh*s.

They'll slap on pasty daylight gazes,
behind flat, fake five-inch lenses.
And their messes'll show.

Let's not let on we're natives.
They'll have us out for looking
loud on them.

WAGGED

We had a fight

it was bruising

you told me
I know nothing of
gender-specific pain

and not as though
I couldn't understand
women but rather
that I didn't get gender

which hurt like bactine

like fumes
in my short hairs
and up behind
my eyes

like bleach with vinegar
hissing from the kitchen

I know enough pain
and thought we were
people to each other
and not these sides

I get sex enough to love it
I get strength enough
to need it

but in this space and
at this time

I am not a chapter
and I am not a plank

this is not the stump
this is fucking *breakfast*.

HERALDED

Come to honor Sad,
a paste and rubbery face,
drooped yet dour eyes—

cast as when, on repeated occasions,
the world rushes up to meet it,
but it does not flinch.

SWIFT

Dozing while Levon hollers,
or strolling through
a mile-round wood,
or asking for a box step.

These were the plans you kept:
three out of three hundred.

You don't lack for talent.
I've held you; I've known you.
Hell, I've been you.

I don't consider you a thief.
I consider you gifted.

A LAST GOODBYE AT WINDSOR LOCKS

You are of a higher plane.
You smile in love. You sigh in pain.
There is no guile about you; no denial.
How seductive. How aspirational.

It explains how you drained the lake.
You drank the fresh water, incomplete.
What's left? I'll eat the fish and snakes,
and you can have the weeds.

It all tastes of brown and black
and gray and rust. I wouldn't lie to you.

Yes, you're incomplete.
Don't be so hurt you can't watch
these stars with me, boots-deep in
mudsuck bed, bellies full
of one fewer day.

Tomorrow, before we go,
show me how to live with knowing
I worked so hard for nothing.

PSALM SUNG WITH HANDS

Ministers, minstrels,
leaners on faith:
here the news is bad.
Here, we spill onto streets.

Picture climbing into a mouth:
one foot on a molar; a heel
spiked on a canine. Hands
tight on the incisors.

Picture climbing into a mouth
so surely that the mouth breaks—
the body splits wide; flips,
and all that's inside

pours, more liquid than human.
That's us become streets.
And all that life that's happened
floats exposed and cold.

We can no sooner
leave the streets
clogged with waste
than sew ourselves back up

and pretend we haven't
once crammed into
another and torn them
in two.

NERVOUS

Your mermaid shaved her head as
a sign of protest:

against lights off a mile-long bridge
sworn to have been crossed on foot;

against a sun-scorched
neck or two; against flaming lips
singing along, sudded and wailed.

Against summer. Summer.
Summer many times seductive.
So when you next hear Willie Dixon,

forget that blonde you loved so much.
Do your best to keep your nerves.
He's a big man, and knows you tried.

WE PARTY

Ripped and rent,
never mended. Still
a bent fender; a dented
bender. Under, asunder.
Plunders appended. Villains
ascended; heroes defended.
Wonders end.
Clipped yet tender. Unattended.

Lenders say it's raining again.
Ten out of ten.

                         AND BULLSHIT

                      (Grew up penned in by chop shops)
                      (and still love to rip shit to shreds)
                      (I crashed a car in Red Hook)
                      (but I now drink less than I think)
                      (I see thieves and cheaters)
                      (thriving by hiding behind saints)
                      (our tricks are a sign of a trend)
                      (speak quick; nip lonely;)

                      (spend and spend)
                      (every night you can)

SAVOY

If I pulled from this catastrophe
careful pages from the spine

then laid them end to end,

they'd reach a town
where lives a woman
in a marigold jacket
and wan-red cord shorts.

She leaches Technicolor
into a gutter of a workday scheme,
plotting endless jailbreaks.

No more jailbreaks.
In a catalogue of honor,
those are demeaning.

INDELICATE DEMANDS

No one is to sleep.
Our eyes are too dry from
recycled air. Let's atrophy right.
Let's massacre a modern masterpiece.

Let us for once pretend
that we do not pretend,

like I pretend the north of France
from the furthest south,
or I pretend a snowbound house,
or I insist on books and books
and books—pretend and insist,
pile them in bed,

and pretend like I'm Hrabal, before
pretending and insisting on one word,
sent in the dark a thousand miles,
meant to mean

that we
do not
pretend.

Let's tear this place apart.

We'll pretend
the dreams we'll miss,
now that we'll stay awake.

My sleepless favorite is
of whisper-thin
lines on blank sheets,
saved for some wilderness,
and clutched
so they slip off the page
when gazing up.

And so we'll pray.

SEPULCHER

Holy Future,
patron saint
of innumerable
chances, damned
to suffer the
battery of vows
and curses
against you,
by both believers
and cheaters:

bleed from your
palms without a
fancy word for it.
Hang hard without
a holiday. Suffer
the done dumb, as
plans made
by mortals dictate.

Masses watch
and pray to age.
You're not of that;
patience isn't kin to age.
It's new life, free of
object permanence.
It's the only child
we won't die
to protect.

LOW LOWLY

Gone go glory
guilty guess tinny mess
ring ring shiny sing

glitter glam crafty
daffy samba sham
Lincoln Sambo am.

Thinking foggy clogged lam
guilty know show best
gone go glory crest

wing wing absent sing
glitter minstrel racy crown
glitter tinsel *tannenbaum*.

ON THE RADIO YESTERDAY

The Hampton Suites in Fairbanks. Digging out the gravel and the snow. Mongoose platypus. Duck-billed mongoose. The best available bourbon. An American prayer. Route 4, Jersey to New York. I can see for miles and miles. Your blonde mane, shock of hair. I want to hear, I hope to tell. Who I thought you were. Sinner. Bearded rapist Philip Marron. There isn't a farm upstate. There was never a farm upstate. Shooting lesbians for love of Jodie Foster. TILE AKA WCOU. The only other conversation. I sing the pogrom electric. Bosom buddies at the D.C. Hilton. Sweaters for the *shtetl*.

Swervewolf.
Beginner swervewolf.

NEXT TIME

It never truly gets dark
because I'm afraid of it;

it's never truly morning
because you're in love with

      [headlights off new mountain passes]

      [mist]

          [the smell of night grass
          and the sound of crickets].

We are distinct;
unique together.

But you're some kind of woman
for me,
so I'll be some kind of man
for you.

ANTIOCH

> Turn around six times,
> spit,
> double-back,
> pray in Esperanto;

give this kit to St. Ignatius.

Tell him the third and
fourth parts
are five times as important
as the first,
and half as important as the seventh.

Esperanto's just for show.
The spitting is key, above all:

> lock in and do it with vigor,
> and let ALL of Antioch know

that I am definitely coming.

ACKNOWLEDGEMENTS

My deep gratitude to the following:

My parents, and to earned family: A. Hughes & N. Adukonis, as well as C. & M. Di Biase; to M. Lange, my best friend.

H. Slatkin, for her tutelage, and for her patience in the face of my developmental lunacy.

H. Mims & Z. Zaus for their kindness, fires, and inspiration.

Assorted bars and taverns, including Uncle Barry's of Park Slope and Frank & Eddie's Butcher Bar of Bay Ridge.

Joan Jett at Southpaw, 2006.

NOTES

Additional inspiration within "This Shelter So Much More" owed to the late David Markson, and the late (and very sincerely missed) Steven Bach.

"Occasioned By Your Thirty-Seventh, Part Four" and "Alabama Lot" appeared in *Other Rooms X*.

COLOPHON

Titles set in Franklin Gothic Book. All the text for which you paid set in Georgia.

Cover art and design by the author, but inspired by art for *Along Came John*, John Patton's debut album as lead performer for Blue Note (BN 84130).

Other versions and more are available at alltimeseastern.com or omniality.com.

Cheers--P.

www.ingramcontent.com/pod-product-compliance
Lightning Source LLC
Chambersburg PA
CBHW032043290426
44110CB00012B/937